DISCOVER BELUGA WHALES

by Kathryn Beaton

Cherry Lake Publishing • Ann Arbor, Michigan

Published in the United States of America
by Cherry Lake Publishing
Ann Arbor, Michigan
www.cherrylakepublishing.com

Content Adviser: William McLellan, research associate, Center for Marine Science, University of North Carolina, Wilmington
Reading Adviser: Marla Conn, ReadAbility, Inc

Photo Credits: © Volt Collection/Shutterstock Images, cover; ©Christopher Meder/Shutterstock Images, 4, 16; © Miles Away Photography/Shutterstock Images, 6; © Vladimir Melnik/Shutterstock Images, 8; © Olkhovsky Nikolay/Shutterstock Images, 10; © Sean Pavone/Shutterstock Images, 12; © Rhianna Brandon/ Shutterstock Images, 14; © Stacy Newman/ Shutterstock Images, 18; © Sparkling Moments Photography/Shutterstock Images, 20

Library of Congress Cataloging-in-Publication Data
Beaton, Kathryn, author.
Discover beluga whales / Kathryn Beaton.
pages cm.—(Splash!)
Summary: "This Level 3 guided reader introduces basic facts about beluga whales, including their physical characteristics, diet, and habitat. Simple call-outs ask the student to think in new ways, supporting inquiry-based reading. Additional text features and search tools, including a glossary and an index, help students locate information and learn new words"— Provided by publisher.
Includes bibliographical references and index.
ISBN 978-1-63362-596-9 (hardcover)—ISBN 978-1-63362-686-7 (pbk.) — ISBN 978-1-63362-776-5 (pdf)—ISBN 978-1-63362-866-3 (ebook)
1. White whale—Juvenile literature. I. Title.

QL737.C433B42 2015
599.5'42—dc23

2014047992

Cherry Lake Publishing would like to acknowledge the work of the Partnership for 21st Century Skills. Please visit www.p21.org for more information.

Printed in the United States of America
Corporate Graphics

TABLE OF CONTENTS

Beluga Bodies

Beluga whales are swimming **mammals**. They are bigger than people but smaller than some other whales. They have large, round heads. A beluga breathes through a **blowhole** on the top of its head.

Belugas have blowholes to let them breathe.

Belugas have small front **flippers** and tail **flukes**, but no fins on their backs. They have thick bodies covered in **blubber**. They have light gray skin. It helps them hide in the ice.

LOOK!

Have you ever seen a beluga whale up close? What other animals does it look like?

Belugas have light gray skin.

A beluga whale sleeps close to the surface of the water. But half of its brain stays awake at a time. This allows the beluga to stay **alert**. Belugas must keep away from **predators** like polar bears and killer whales.

Polar bears sometimes hunt beluga whales.

Very Hungry Whales

Belugas love to eat octopuses, squid, and fish. Belugas have wide mouths with small teeth. Often, they swallow their food without chewing.

MAKE A GUESS!

How does the shape and size of a beluga's mouth help it eat the foods it likes? Write down a guess. Go online to see if you're right.

Belugas' teeth are not very sharp.

Belugas need to eat lots of food to stay healthy. An adult beluga might weight 3,000 pounds. Sometimes belugas hunt in deep water. Sometimes they hunt near **shallow** coastlines.

Belugas need a lot of food to keep their huge bodies healthy.

Belugas mostly live in the **Arctic Ocean**. The water is cold and shallow. There are many belugas near Canada, Russia, and the United States (Alaska). They swim in big groups.

The Cook Inlet, in Alaska, is famous for all the belugas that live there.

Big, Playful Babies

A beluga baby, or **calf**, is dark gray. As it grows up, its skin turns lighter. The calf can already swim when it is born. It stays with its mother for a couple of years.

A beluga baby needs milk from its mother.

The belugas in the Cook Inlet, in Alaska, are **endangered**. Belugas in other places are not endangered. Some are kept in **captivity**, where scientists study and care for them.

THINK!

Beluga whale trainers start their work early in the morning. They feed the whales and clean up messes. They also perform in shows with the belugas. Go online to find out more about trainers. Do you think that the bad parts of the job balance the good parts? Why or why not?

Beluga whales are common in water parks.

Beluga whales are very playful. They like to sing to each other. People can visit belugas in **aquariums**. There, they can see belugas swim, and they can listen to beluga songs.

Visitors to aquariums can enjoy watching the belugas.

Think About It

Go online to watch videos of beluga whales. What do you notice? How do the whales' bodies compare to the way they are described in this book?

Belugas have very light skin. What things might happen if they had colorful patterns?

Ask your parents or teacher if you can visit an aquarium to see a beluga whale. Before you go, write down what you think you will see. When you return home, write down what you saw.

Find Out More

BOOK

Rake, Jody Sullivan. *Beluga Whales Up Close.* North Mankato, MN: Capstone Press, 2009.

WEB SITE

World Wildlife Fund—Beluga Whale

www.worldwildlife.org/species/beluga

This site has photos and information about how beluga whales are being threatened and how you can help.

Glossary

alert (uh-LURT) paying attention and ready to act

aquariums (uh-KWAIR-ee-uhmz) places for visitors to see ocean animals

Arctic Ocean (AHRK-tik OH-shuhyn) the water around the North Pole

blowhole (BLO-hole) a hole at the top of a beluga's head through which it breathes air

blubber (BLUHB-ur) a thick layer of fat under the beluga's skin

calf (KAF) a baby beluga whale

captivity (kap-TIV-i-tee) being held or trapped by people

endangered (en-DAYN-jurd) in danger of dying out

flippers (FLIP-urz) the wide flat fins that help whales swim

flukes (FLOOKS) the two halves of the beluga's tail

mammals (MAM-uhlz) animals that are wam-blooded, give birth to live babies, make milk, and breathe air

predators (PRED-uh-turz) animals that live by hunting other animals to eat

shallow (SHAL-oh) not deep

Index

About the Author

Kathryn Beaton lives and writes in Ann Arbor, Michigan.